A Picture Dictionary of the Bible

By RUTH P. TUBBY

Illustrated by RUTH KING

Abingdon

NASHVILLE

5527

COPYRIGHT 1949 BY PIERCE AND SMITH
ALL RIGHTS RESERVED. PRINTED IN U. S. A.

ISBN 0-687-31411-9
Library of Congress Catalog Number 49-7743

THE AUTHOR wishes to express her thanks for their gracious and inestimable help in checking definitions and pictures to Dr. Samuel J. Terrien, Associate Professor of Old Testament, Union Theological Seminary; Rabbi Bernard Mandelbaum, Registrar of the Rabbinical School, The Jewish Theological Seminary of America; and Rev. William J. Gibbons, S.J., Executive Secretary, Catholic Children's Book Club.

She wishes also to mention five outstanding source books which were of great value in the preparation of A PICTURE DICTIONARY OF THE BIBLE: *Dictionary of the Bible,* by James Hastings (Scribners); *The Exhaustive Concordance of the Bible,* by James Strong (Abingdon-Cokesbury); *Encyclopedia of Bible Life,* by M. S. and J. L. Miller (Harper); *The Bible Guide Book,* by Mary Entwistle (Abingdon-Cokesbury); and *Daily Life in Bible Times,* by Albert E. Bailey (Scribners).

To my mother

for her unfailing inspiration and encouragement

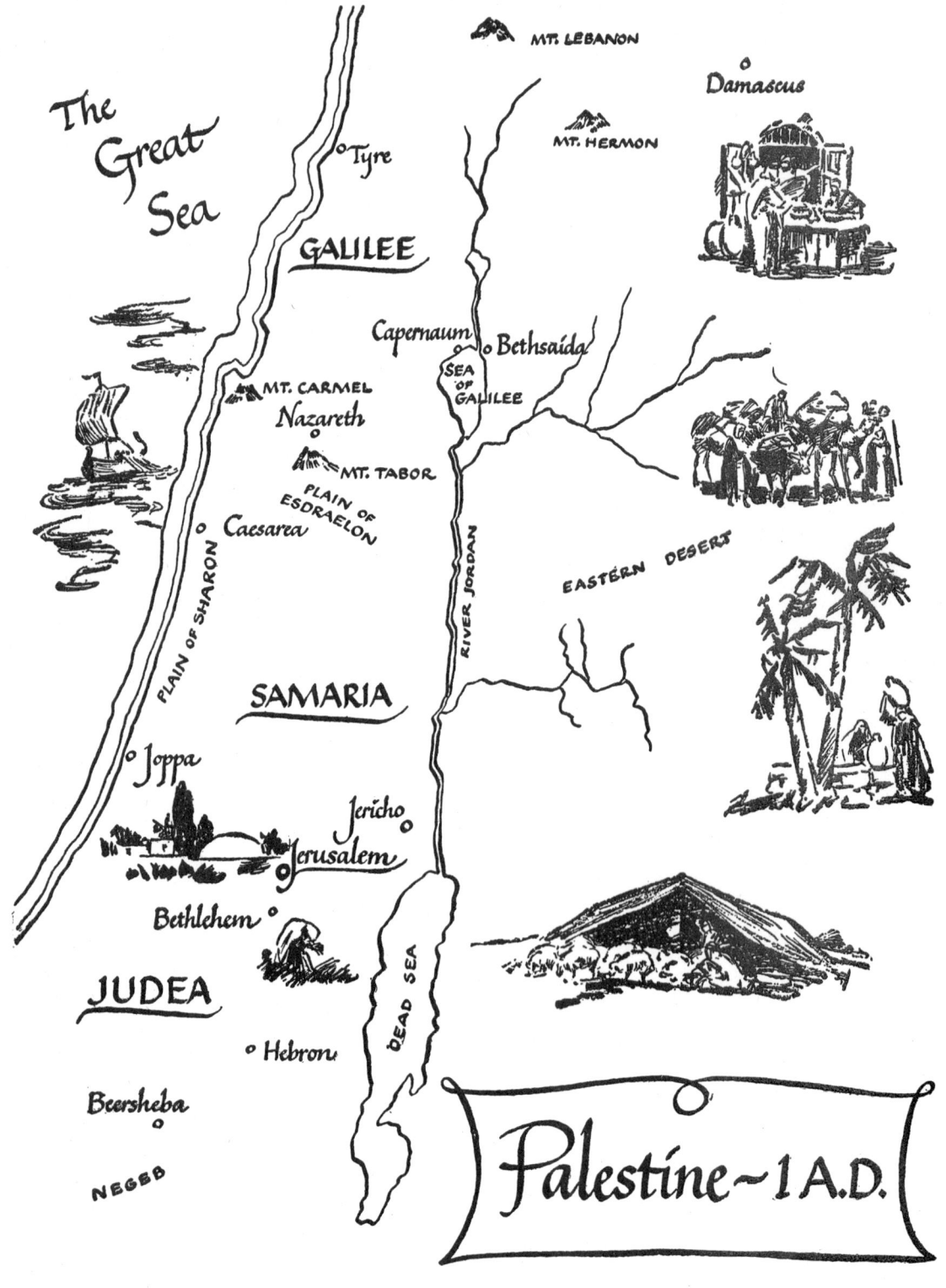

A Picture Dictionary of the Bible

abiding
Lasting for a long time, or staying with or near a person or place

abode
See dwelling place

abomination
A wicked action or thing which causes disgust or hatred

abundance
A large amount or great supply

adder
A small poisonous snake

ADDER

alabaster
A beautiful stone, usually cloudy white but sometimes with touches of red, yellow, or gray. Boxes, vases, and other ornaments are carved out of alabaster.

ALABASTER

Almighty
God, the all powerful

almond tree
A small tree with flowers like a peach blossom. The fruit is a nut which is used in many different ways, mainly for food and flavoring.

ALMOND TREE

alms
Money, food, or clothing given to beggars and poor people

aloes
Fragrant perfume, made from the oil in the bark of the aloe plant

altar
A pile of stones or a raised platform used in Bible days as a place where sacrifices were made. In modern churches and synagogues it is the raised place for a holy part of the service in the worship of God.

ALTAR

amen
The word repeated at the end of a prayer or religious statement to show the belief of the person who has spoken it. Amen means "So be it."

angel
A heavenly being

anoint
To pour or apply oil on a person or thing as part of a sacred ceremony

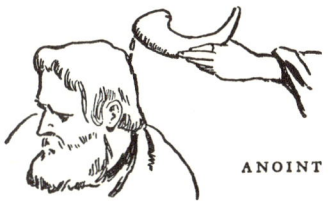
ANOINT

anklet
A ring fastened around the ankle. When several were worn, they jingled at every step.

ANKLET

apostle
A special messenger or follower sent out to preach the teachings of his master

apparel
Clothing or dress

ark
A chest, especially the one used to hold the tablets of stone on which the Ten Commandments were written. Also the boat on which Noah and his family escaped the flood.

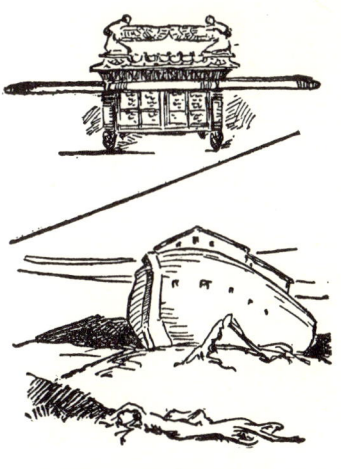
ARK

armor

A covering of metal, worn to protect the body in battle. In Bible times men wore shields, breastplates, and helmets as armor.

arrayed

Dressed. A woman arrayed herself to go out by putting a veil over her head and a cloak over her other garments.

ARMOR

ass

See donkey

atonement

"At-one-ment." Bringing persons into right relationship or agreement, especially after one has been wronged by the other. Satisfaction to God for sin.

AVENGER

avenger

A man who punishes others for the trouble they have made or for the suffering they have caused

balm
A healing oil used to cure pain; comfort brought to a person in trouble. Balm of Gilead had a pleasant odor and women used it as a skin cream.

banquet
A feast or party with plenty of good food, usually ending with speeches or other entertainment

BANQUET

baptism
A religious ceremony of admission to a church; the sacred Christian ceremony of initiation

barley
The seed or grain of a cereal grass which is used as a food for people and animals

battering-ram
A large beam of wood with an iron head, used in ancient times to knock down the wall of a city being attacked

BATTERING-RAM

beckon
To call someone by a signal made with the hand or head

befall
To happen

BECKON

beggar
A very poor person who has to ask for everything he needs

behold
Look! See!

BEGGAR

benefits
Deeds of kindness which help improve people's lives or make them happier

beseech
To ask earnestly for a special favor or blessing

birthright
The rights or privileges which a child in a family, usually the oldest, has by law and custom. Esau sold his birthright to his brother Jacob.

blasphemy
Speaking evil of God or sacred things

blemish
A spot or mark of injury which spoils the appearance

blessing
The act of bestowing good will or other favors. Often God is asked to give blessings to his people.

bondage
Slavery. A bondman or bondwoman is one who has to work for and serve a master for many years, sometimes for his or her entire lifetime.

BONDAGE

booty
Prizes seized in war; usually goods taken from the enemy by force

BOOTY

bounty
Kindness in giving freely; a reward for a special act or piece of work

brasen
> Brass; made of brass

breastplate
> A metal plate worn over the upper part of the body to protect it in battle

BREASTPLATE

brethren
> Brothers; near relatives or close friends

buckler
> A shield worn on the arm to protect the body in battle; something which protects or defends

buffet
> To strike or slap

bullock
> An ox or young bull

BULLOCK

burnt offering
> Something burnt on an altar as a sacrifice or gift to a god or to an idol

caldron

A large kettle or pot

CALDRON

candlestick

A tall stand or a low dish with a small cup in it to hold a candle. Often candlesticks are made of precious metals. The seven-branched golden candlestick used in Jewish worship has special religious meaning.

CANDLESTICK

captivity

Being a prisoner. A captive is a person who is taken as a prisoner in war and held by force.

caravan

A group of travelers making a long trip, usually through a desert. Caravans often have camels and donkeys to carry their baggage.

CARAVAN

casting net

A round net which is thrown into the water to catch fish.

cedar

A large evergreen tree with reddish, sweet-smelling wood. Buildings made of cedar last a long time because the wood is so strong. The cedars of Lebanon were especially famous in Bible times.

CEDAR

censer

A cup-shaped container for perfume or incense. When the incense is burned in certain services of worship, the censers are swung back and forth.

CENSER

centurion

A captain who commanded a hundred men. The Roman army was made up of many such companies.

CENTURION

ceremony

A solemn act or service

chaff

The covering or husks of seeds and grasses which is left after the grain has been threshed out. The word is also used for something that is light and has no real value.

charger

A large plate or platter

CHARGER

chariot

A low two-wheeled cart drawn by horses. Ancient peoples used chariots in races and processions and in war.

CHARIOT

chasten

To punish in order to make better

chastisement

Punishment

cherub

A heavenly being. Two or more are called cherubim.

chronicle

A story of historical happenings, arranged in the order in which they took place

cistern

A tank used to keep water. Often these tanks are set below the ground to catch rain water from the roof above.

cleave

To cling to; also to separate or divide

cloak

A long loose coat that covers a man or woman

CLOAK

cock

A rooster. The cock's crow in the early morning was often the sound which woke people up.

COCK

coin

A small piece of metal which shows by marks on it that it has value as money

COINS

commandment

An order given by someone who has power; in the Bible, usually by God. Moses received the Ten Commandments from God.

communion
A close spiritual tie or bond

consecrate
To set apart for a holy purpose

cooking vessel
A pan or kettle in which food is cooked. Usually it is made of metal or earthenware.

COOKING VESSELS

coppersmith
A man who makes all kinds of cooking vessels and utensils out of copper

corrupt
Rotten; evil; to make wicked or bad

COPPERSMITH

covenant
A solemn agreement or promise made between two or more people

17

covetousness
Envy or greed which makes a person eager to get something he does not have, especially something which belongs to another person

crucifixion
The act of killing a person by nailing or binding his hands and feet to a cross. Jesus was crucified on a hill named Golgotha.

cruse
A pot or cup or wide bottle for holding liquids

CRUSE

cummin
A weedlike plant, similar to parsley. Its seeds were used for flavoring.

cubit
An ancient measure of length, from 17 to 21 inches

cupbearer
A servant who fills the cups when drink is served

CUPBEARER

cymbals

A musical instrument—two hollow brass plates, with handles on the outside. The plates are struck together to make a ringing sound.

CYMBALS

cypress

A kind of evergreen tree which usually grows tall and straight

date palm

A tall tree with small flowers and with long leaves shaped like feathers. Dates form in clusters near the top of the trunk. The sweet sap and the stem fibers can be used as well as the fruit.

dayspring

The dawn or the earliest part of the day

decree

An order from someone in power

CYPRESS

DATE PALM

dedicate
> *See* consecrate

defile
> To make unclean

devout
> Religious; devoted

DISCIPLE

disciple
> A pupil or follower. A person who accepts the teaching of his master and goes out to teach others. The twelve disciples were Jesus' closest followers.

distaff
> The staff for holding the flax or wool from which the thread is drawn for spinning

DISTAFF

donkey
> A small, strong animal with long ears. People use donkeys to carry heavy loads and to ride. In Bible times a man who owned a donkey was thought to be well off.

DONKEY

dove

A small pigeon, thought of as the symbol of peace

DOVE

dowry

The money or goods which a woman brings to her husband at the time of their marriage, or which a man pays to his bride's father

dram

A weight—a small part of an ounce

dungeon

A dark room, usually underground, where prisoners are kept

DUNGEON

dwelling place

The house or building where a person or family lives

dyeing

Changing the color of a thing by dipping it into a colored liquid

eagle
A large bird which flies fast and sees very far

EAGLE

ebony
A hard black wood

elder
A person who, because of his age, becomes a ruler or a judge or a leader of people

ephod
A robe for the Jewish high priest. It was usually embroidered and fastened by a girdle.

EPHOD

epistle
A letter. Several books in the New Testament are epistles.

EPISTLE

evangelist
A preacher or messenger of the gospel

eventide
Evening

ewe lamb
A young sheep

exalt
To lift up; to praise

exile
Forced absence from home or country

extortion
Taking something from a person against his will

EWE LAMB

EXTORTION

famine
A time when there is almost no food and when everyone is **hungry**

farthing
A coin of very small value

fast.
   The act of going without food, usually for religious reasons

feast
   A religious festival or celebration, usually with eating; the opposite of a fast

FEAST

fellowship
   Friendly feeling between persons with the same interests

fetter
   A chain or band which binds the feet so that they can hardly move

FETTER

fig tree
   A tree with very large green leaves and a small round fruit which can be eaten fresh or dried

FIG TREE

firmament
   The heavens or the whole circle of the sky

first fruit

The first grain gathered at harvesttime. This was often given to God as a thank offering.

FIRST FRUIT

fitches

Black seeds, something like peas, used as medicine or flavoring. They grow on vines in the grainfields and have to be separated from the grain at harvesttime

flail

A wooden stick with a short thick piece fastened at the bottom to swing from it. This is used to beat grain from the chaff.

FLAIL

flax

A slender plant with bright blue flowers. The fiber from the dried stems makes linen thread. The seeds are used for medicine and oils.

fleece

The coat of wool that covers a sheep

25

flock
A group of animals, birds, or people

flute
A long hollow tube with holes in the side. Different musical sounds are made by blowing through one hole and putting fingers over one or more of the others.

FLOCK   FLUTE

forbear
To keep from doing something; to be patient

forerunner
A messenger or person sent ahead to tell of the coming of others. John the Baptist was the forerunner of Jesus.

forsake
To give up

fountain
A spring of water which rises out of the earth

fowl
Any bird, especially large edible birds, including chickens

frankincense
A sweet-smelling gum containing so much oil that it could be burned. It was highly prized because it could be used in many different ways. The Wise Men brought a gift of frankincense to the baby Jesus.

fugitive
A man who runs away because he is in danger

furlong
A measure of length—one-eighth of a mile

furrow
A trench in the earth, made by a plow

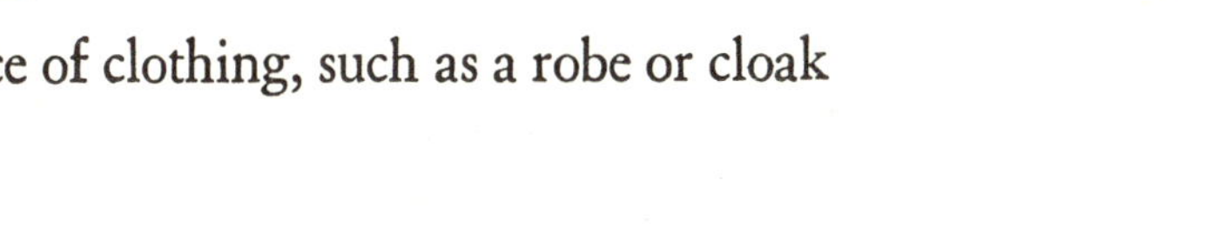

FUGITIVE

FURROW

garment
A piece of clothing, such as a robe or cloak

garner
A storehouse for grain; to gather grain from the fields

gate
An opening in a wall or fence. In ancient times cities were surrounded by high walls and the gates in them were closed at night to protect the people from enemies outside.

GATE

gazelle
A small swift deer

gird
To dress or get ready

girdle
A wide belt which goes around the body at the waist

gleaning
Gathering the grain left by the reapers in a field

GLEANING

glorify
To worship or praise

goad

A pointed stick used to spur an animal

GOAD

goatskin

The skin of a goat or the leather made from it. Goatskins were often used to hold water or milk.

GOATSKIN

GOLDSMITH

goldsmith

A man who makes fine dishes and ornaments from gold

goodman

The head of a family; the master of a house

gospel

Good news. In the New Testament it refers to the record of Christ's life and teachings and to the teachings themselves

GOURD

gourd

A vegetable which can be dried and hollowed out for a cup or bowl

granary
A storehouse for grain

graven
Carved. The Ten Commandments were graven on stone.

grudge
The bitter feeling which one person may have for another when he thinks he has been wronged

habitation
See dwelling place

hallelujah
Praise ye the Lord!

handmaid
A woman servant

HARP

harp
A musical instrument with strings set in a frame

harvest
A crop of grain or fruit; the act of picking it

headdress
A covering or decoration for the head

HEADDRESS

hearth

The floor of brick, stone, or clay on which a fire is made. There is usually a chimney, through which the smoke can go out, leading up from it.

HEARTH

hearken

Listen

heathen

People who do not believe in the true God

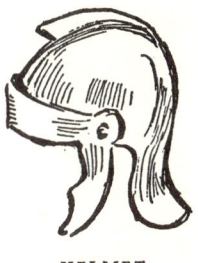

HELMET

helmet

A metal covering worn to protect the head in battle

herb

A seed plant used for medicine or flavor or fragrance

heritage

Something precious which is inherited; the property which comes from a father to his children

hewer
A man who chops wood with an ax

HEWER

hireling
A man who works for pay

honeycomb
A group of tiny wax cells made by bees, in which they store their honey

hosanna
A shout of praise

host
A large number of people gathered together

HUSBANDMAN

husbandman
A farmer or the master of a house

hyssop
An herb that smells like mint. Its leaves were used to heal bruises.

HYSSOP

32

idol

A picture or image of a person or thing used as an object of worship. It is often carved from wood or stone.

IDOL

image

A picture or statue of someone or something; sometimes an idol

incense

The perfume or smoke which comes from gums or spices as they burn

INCENSE

iniquity

Evil or wrong doing; injustice

inkhorn

A small horn bottle to hold ink

INKHORN

inn

A hotel or building where a person can eat or sleep

ivory

The hard white substance which forms the tusks of elephants and other animals

33

jackal
A wild dog, smaller than a wolf

JACKAL

jar
A tall container of earthenware or glass in which fruits or vegetables were stored. *See* waterpot

JAR

jubilee
A time of joy

jubilee year
A religious celebration of the Jews, observed every fifty years

judgment seat
The chair or bench on which a judge sat in court

kine
Cows or cattle

KINE

kinsmen
Men of the same family or race; relatives; also called kindred

34

lamentation
Loud cries of grief

lamp
A bowl or cup which holds a wick in oil. When lighted, it burns brightly.

LAMP

latchet
A narrow leather strap by which a shoe or sandal is fastened to the foot

LATCHET

lattice
A framed network of crossed strips of wood or metal

LATTICE

lawgiver
One who makes a law

leaven
Something, like yeast, used to make dough rise

lentil
A vegetable with large flat seeds, like peas or beans

LENTIL

leprosy
A serious skin disease. Lepers were outcasts in Bible times.

lintel
   The crosspiece above a door

lo
   Behold! See!

locust
   A grasshopper. Often locusts travel in huge swarms and eat all the plants and the leaves of trees.

loom
   A frame on which thread is woven into cloth

lyre
   A stringed musical instrument similar to a harp

magnify
   To praise highly

manger
   An open box in which food is placed for horses and cattle. Jesus was born in a manger.

manifold
   Many

manna
> Food or nourishment supplied by God. The Israelites ate manna while in the wilderness.

mantle
> *See* cloak

market place
> An open place in a town where people bring food and clothing to buy and sell

MARKET PLACE

mattock
> A pick or hoe used for digging

MATTOCK

measure
> A container known to hold an exact amount of dry things or liquids

MEASURE

measuring reed
> A tall bending grass used as a measure of length

mediator
> A peacemaker

merchant
A man who makes his living by buying and selling

Messiah
The expected savior and deliverer of the Hebrew people

MERCHANT

millet
A grain used for cereal or food for animals

millstones
Two large rounded stones between which grain is ground into flour

ministry
Service to others

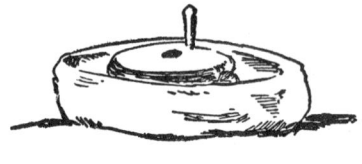

MILLSTONES

miracle
A happening which is so strange and wonderful that it cannot be explained in any usual way; a special act of God

mite
A small coin

moneychanger
A man who makes his living by exchanging different kinds of money

mortar

A small strong cup or bowl in which substances are pounded or ground with a pestle

MORTAR

mud brick

A square piece of mud dried and hardened in the sun, used to build simple houses

multitude

Many people or things gathered together; a crowd

mustard seed

The tiny seed of the mustard plant. These seeds are ground into powder for seasoning.

myrrh

A sweet, brownish gum, used in incense and perfumes. Myrrh was brought by the Wise Men as a gift to the baby Jesus.

myrtle tree

A small evergreen tree. Its flowers, leaves, and berries were used to make perfume, and carpenters valued its wood.

MYRTLE TREE

nomad
A man who has no settled home; a wanderer

oasis
A green spot in the desert where water can be found

OASIS   NOMAD

oblation
A religious offering

observance
The act of obeying a law or custom

offspring
A child or children; descendant

ointment
A soft cream or salve to be rubbed on the skin to soothe or **heal it**

olive tree

A low-growing tree with small gray-green leaves. Its fruit can be eaten green or ripe or made into oil.

OLIVE TREE

omnipotent

All-powerful

onyx

A semi-precious stone with different colored layers

ordained

Appointed, or decided by God

ordinance

A rule or a law

ox

A large, slow-moving animal used in farm work, especially to draw heavy loads

OX

palace
A fine, large house where a king or ruler lives

palm tree
A tall tropical tree with many feather-shaped leaves at the top. It is especially valuable for its oil. *See also* date palm

PALACE

palsy
A disease which causes a person to shake

parable
A short story from which a lesson may be learned. Jesus told many parables.

paradise
A beautiful and delightful place; heaven

parching
Drying. Grain is parched by lying in the sun.

PARCHING

parchment
The skin of a sheep or goat or other animal dried in such a way that one can write on it

Passover
An annual feast of the Jews in celebration of their deliverance from Egypt

pasture
A field where animals feed on growing grass or grain

PASTURE

patriarch
The father or ruler of a family or tribe

PATRIARCH

Pentecost
A religious harvesttime festival of the Jews, seven weeks after the Passover

peradventure
Perhaps; possibly

persecution
Hurting or killing people, usually because something about them, such as their religion, is different from the one in common use

pestilence
Any disease which spreads quickly and causes great suffering among many people; a plague

pestle
A small club-shaped tool used to pound things up very fine

PESTLE

petition
Request

pilgrimage
A journey made to a sacred place

PILGRIMAGE

pillar
A tall post built to hold the weight of a roof or beam

pipe
A musical instrument something like a flute. Shepherds used their pipes to call their flocks together.

plague
See pestilence

PLOWSHARE

plowshare
The pointed part of a plow which cuts into the ground and turns it over to make a furrow

pomegranate
A thick-skinned tropical fruit. It is scarlet and somewhat like an orange. It has many seeds and is eaten raw.

POMEGRANATE

pottage
Thick soup or stew

potter
A man who makes dishes and jars from clay. Potters often use a turning wheel to round out bowls and vases.

POTTER

precept
A command or order

priest
A special servant of God who leads the people in religious services

principality
A small state, governed by a prince

privily
Privately

prodigal
A person who wastes his money or belongings. Jesus told a story of a prodigal son and his father.

prophet
One chosen by God to speak for him. Isaiah, Jeremiah, Amos, Micah, and Ezekiel were some of the prophets of Old Testament days.

provender
Feed for animals

prudent
Sensible; wise

PROPHET

pruning hook
A long pole with a curved blade, often used to cut off branches

PRUNING HOOK

psalm
A religious song or poem for use in worship. One of the books of the Old Testament is made up of psalms.

psaltery
A harplike musical instrument

PSALTERY

publican
A man who collected taxes

PUBLICAN

quail
A small brown bird that lives in open fields and is used for food

quench
To put an end to, as to extinguish a fire or to satisfy thirst

rabbi
The English form of the Hebrew word for teacher or master

raiment
Clothing

RAM

ram
A male sheep

rampart
A broad embankment around a place which is fortified against attack

raven
A large black bird like a crow

RAVEN

47

reaper
One who cuts or harvests grain in the fields

recompense
To repay or to reward

REAPER

redeemer
One who saves others from sin and suffering; the title applied to Jesus by Christians

reed
A tall grass with hollow stem. Reeds are used to cover the roofs of houses, as musical instruments, and in many other ways. *See also* measuring reed

refiner
A person who purifies metal

REEDS

refuge
A place where a person can find shelter or safety

remission
Forgiveness

rending
Tearing a thing apart with great effort

repent
> To feel sorry for something one has done or failed to do and to resolve to do better

resurrection
> The act of living again or rising after death. On Easter Christians celebrate the resurrection of Jesus.

revile
> To abuse with words

righteous
> Free from wrong; right

robe
> *See* cloak

rod
> A long thin stick

ROD

Sabbath
> A day of rest. For the Jewish people, the seventh day of the week; for most Christians, the first day of the week.

sackcloth
> Coarse, dark cloth made of goat's or camel's hair. It was worn as a sign of grief.

SACKCLOTH

sacrifice

An offering to a god, usually made at an altar; also, to give up something. In Bible days cattle, sheep, and doves were often sacrificed to God.

SACRIFICE

salvation

The saving of people from evil, especially from wrongdoing

sanctify

To make holy

sanctuary

A holy place; a place of refuge

sandal

A kind of shoe with the sole strapped to the foot by a latchet

SANDALS

savior

A person who saves others from danger and death; the title applied to Jesus by Christians

scapegoat
One who bears the blame for others

scribe
A clerk who writes for other people or keeps their records

scrip
A small bag or wallet, often used by shepherds

scripture
Sacred writings; the Bible

scroll
A roll of parchment with writing on it

seal
A design carved into a substance so that it can be transferred to another softer substance, or the print made by the design; to mark with a design; to close tightly

seer
A wise man who can look into the future

selah
A word used in the Psalms to indicate a pause

sepulchre
A place of burial; a tomb

SEPULCHRE

serpent
A snake, usually a large one

sheaf
A bundle of stalks of grain tied together

SHEAF

shearing
Cutting the fleece from sheep

sheepfold
A shelter or pen for sheep

shekel
An ancient coin

shepherd
A man who tends and guards sheep

SHEEPFOLD

shield
A large piece of metal held in the hand and used in battle to protect the body

sickle
A curved metal blade attached to a handle, used to cut grass and grain

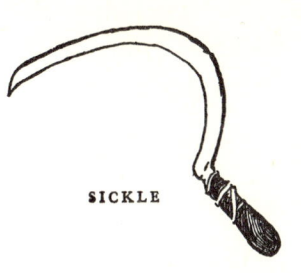

SICKLE

siege
The camping of an army in front of a fortified place in order to force its surrender

silversmith
One who makes utensils and jewelry out of silver

sleeping mat
A long pad, made of soft material, such as woven straw, which is spread on the floor or ground to sleep on

SLEEPING MAT

sling
A small hand device for throwing stones

sluggard
A lazy person

smite
To strike a person or thing, usually with the hand or with a weapon held in the hand

snare
A trap for catching birds or animals

sojourner
A traveler who stays in one place for a short time only

soothsayer
One who tells what is going to happen

sorcerer
A magician

sowing
Planting or scattering seed on the ground

spinning
Drawing out and twisting wool and flax into thread

staff
A long piece of wood; a pole or rod. A shepherd's staff had a curved end.

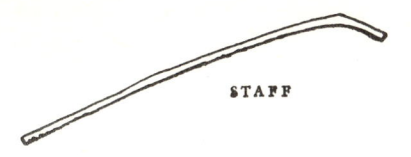

stall
A shelter or pen for horses and cattle

staves
Sticks

steward
A manager; a man who takes care of his master's property, collects money for him, and gives orders to the servants

stranger
A person who is not known; often one who comes from another place

suffer
To allow; to endure pain

supplication
An earnest request

swaddling clothes
Strips of cloth wrapped around a tiny baby

sycamore tree
A shade tree with a fig-like fruit

SWADDLING CLOTHES

synagogue
The building which Jews use for meeting, study, and worship

tabernacle
A temporary dwelling place; a tent used by Jews as a place of worship, which could be moved from one place to another

TABERNACLE

tablet
A flat piece of hard material on which a person can write or draw

tabret
A small drum; a timbrel

talent
An ancient coin of great value

tare
A weed which grows in grainfields

taxgatherer
A man who collects money for taxes

temple
A place of worship

tentmaker
One who makes tents. In Bible times he used the skins of animals or thick woven cloth.

TEMPLE

TENTMAKER

testament
A solemn act, agreement, or promise. The first part of the Bible is called the Old Testament; the second part, the New Testament.

testimony
A solemn speech made to prove a fact; a sworn statement

thank offering
A religious gift made to show thanks

thong
A strip of leather, often used to fasten sandals, or at the end of a whip

thorn
A sharp spike that sticks out of some plants or trees

threshing
Beating grain out of its sheaf by treading, rubbing, or by striking it with a flail

THRESHING

threshold
The piece of wood or stone under a door; a doorsill

THRESHOLD

throng
A crowd of people. *See also* multitude

tidings
A piece of news; a message

tilling
Plowing the earth, planting seed, and cultivating a crop

TILLING

timbrel
A small drum beaten by hand

tithe
A tenth part

TIMBREL

tomb
See sepulchre

trample
To step heavily or stamp. Grass is trampled by cattle.

transgressor
A person who breaks the law; a sinner

trespass
To do wrong; to go onto another's property without permission

trial
The act of testing a person to find out if he has done wrong

tribe
A group of people descended from the same ancestor, with the same religion and language

tribulation
Trouble

trumpet
A musical instrument with a long metal tube and a bell-shaped end. It is blown through a cuplike mouthpiece.

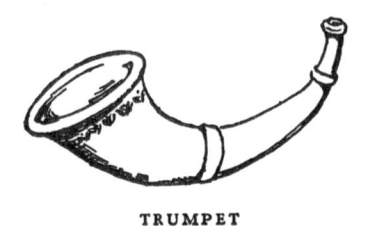

TRUMPET

tumult
The noise made by a crowd of people

TUMULT

turtledove
See dove

usurer
One who lends money and charges interest for its use

uttermost
Farthest; most distant

vengeance
Punishment in return for an injury or wrong

verily
Truly

vessel
See cooking vessel

vesture
See clothing

vineyard
The place where grapes are grown

vintage
A year's harvest of grapes

viper
A poisonous snake; a spiteful person

vision
A sight seen as in a dream, not with the eyes

visitation
A visit, especially an official visit; a reward or punishment sent by God

wailing
Weeping or mourning loudly. The Wailing Wall in Jerusalem is the place where the Jews go to mourn.

WAILING

wares
Goods; merchandise to be bought or sold

WARES

waste
A desert or wilderness; destruction, as by war

waterpot
A jar in which water is kept or carried. It was often used to carry water from wells.

weaver
One who makes yarn into cloth

well
A hole dug in the earth to reach a supply of water; a spring or fountain

wilderness
An uncultivated region where few people live. The Israelites lived for many years in the wilderness between Egypt and Palestine.

wine press
Where the juice is pressed out of grapes for wine

winnowing
Separating the grain from the chaff with a fan or flail

witness
One who has knowledge of a fact or event and testifies about it

woe
    Grief or trouble

wound
    An injury on the body of a person or animal, especially one caused by violence

yield
    To give; to produce

yoke
    A bar of wood by which oxen draw loads; a burden

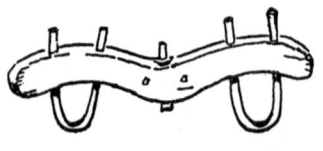

YOKE

zeal
    Eagerness; enthusiasm